GIFTED & TALENTED®

*To develop
your child's gifts
and talents*

STORY STARTERS

Stories About Animals

By Julie Koerner

Illustrated by Leo Abbett

LOWELL HOUSE JUVENILE

LOS ANGELES

CONTEMPORARY BOOKS

CHICAGO

For Matt and Jenna.
                        — J.K.

Reviewed and endorsed by Susan C. Hay, M.A.,
veteran educator and elementary reading and curriculum specialist

GIFTED & TALENTED® STORY STARTERS: Stories About Animals will help develop your child's natural talents and gifts by providing story-telling and writing activities to enhance critical and creative thinking skills. These skills of logic and reasoning teach children **how** to think. They are precisely the skills emphasized by teachers of gifted and talented children.

Thinking skills are the skills needed to be able to learn anything at any time. Unlike events, words, and teaching methods, thinking skills never change. If a child has a grasp of how to think, school success and even success in life will become more assured. In addition, the child will become self-confident as he or she approaches new tasks with the ability to think them through and discover solutions.

GIFTED & TALENTED® STORY STARTERS: Stories About Animals presents these skills in a unique way, combining the basic subject areas of reading and language arts with thinking skills. The top of each page is labeled to indicate the specific thinking skill developed. Here are some of the skills you will find:

- Deduction — the ability to reach a logical conclusion by interpreting clues

- Understanding Relationships — the ability to recognize how objects, shapes, and words are similar or dissimilar; to classify or categorize

- Sequencing — the ability to organize events, numbers; to recognize patterns

- Inference — the ability to reach a logical conclusion from given or assumed evidence

- Creative Thinking — the ability to generate unique ideas; to compare and contrast the same elements in different situations; to present imaginative solutions to problems

GIFTED & TALENTED® STORY STARTERS: Stories About Animals uses a variety of different exercises to help your child develop his or her creative writing and creative thinking skills.

The Fill-in-the-Blank Exercises at the beginning of this book will help your child gain confidence in the story-telling (and story-writing) process. The child has two choices: **a)** to select words from the appropriate Word Lists to drop into the blank spaces; **b)** to use other words or phrases of his or her own choosing to fill in the blanks.

Using the Word Lists expands the young child's concept of what makes a "good" story. With the Word Lists, the hero can be a girl or a boy, a duck, or even a kitchen appliance. It is recommended that the Word Lists be used first, and that you read the stories with your child again, after all the blanks have been filled in. Once the child feels comfortable with the creative freedom to tell his or her own stories, the Fill-in-the-Blank Exercises can be reused, with your child providing new words for the blanks.

To help your child grasp the "purpose" and "place" of certain words (like adjectives and nouns), read words to the child from the lists, then ask the child to make up his or her own words instead, words "like" the ones on the lists. Going over the exercises reinforces not only the function of language but its richness as well.

It is important not to be judgmental about your child's choices. The Word Lists reflect the variety of language, so that the child does not form too narrow or too rigid a concept of what is "properly" a hero or "properly" a descriptive word. A child who rejects a Word List and chooses to describe a morning as "yellow" and the hero as "a doorknob" has a very interesting story in the works.

In the first half of the book you will find Eye-Opening Descriptive Exercises, which encourage your child to use his or her observation skills. Through the use of questions, the activities teach your child to mine his or her own experiences and observations for story ideas.

Sight is the most well-developed observatory sense, but children should draw on all five of their senses as they describe and make observations about each picture in the Eye-Opening Descriptive Exercises. This will help your child develop a rich and well-rounded ability to write descriptions. As your child looks at a picture and makes observations about it, ask your child questions to draw out even more detail.

After your child completes the Fill-in-the-Blank Exercises and the Eye-Opening Descriptive Exercises, he or she will develop an "ear, eye, nose, taste, and touch" for telling a story. The child will then be ready for Write the Middle and Write the Ending Exercises. Here, stories are started for the child, and the child then has to provide either the middle or the ending. To help your child through the middle of a story, remember that this part of a story is a link that provides a logical chain of events from the beginning (provided) to the end (provided). So ask the child to read the ending out loud and imagine what could have happened to lead to such an ending. To help your child through the ending exercises, ask him or her to imagine more than one way the story can conclude. The more children use their imaginations, the more they will move away from clichéd endings and into creative endings.

The final section contains Advanced Exercises. These provide little help in the creation and writing of each story. The child is given scenarios for stories, or is asked to use words in a Word Box, but unlike the earlier exercises, no portion of a story is provided. Please encourage your child to consider his or her initial effort as a first draft. Once he or she has completed an Advanced Exercise and some time has passed, ask the child to expand on the first attempt on another piece of paper. You will both be surprised at how effortlessly the second (and third) drafts become more complete, and even more interesting, stories.

Participate with and read to your child. Help him or her with harder words. A child's imagination should not be limited only to those words he or she can read, since children understand the meaning of words even if they cannot read them. The same is true for those words they cannot write. If necessary, record your child's stories for him or her. Regardless of whether your child can write full, complete sentences, the child will gain much from this book. Exercising the imagination is what **GIFTED & TALENTED STORY STARTERS** is all about.

Good luck, have fun, and remember: Good writers read, so go to the library often with your child.

Look carefully at the picture. Then fill in the blanks to tell a story about the picture. Match the numbers under the blank lines to the Word Lists on the next page. Choose words from the lists or use your own words to help you complete the story. After you finish, read your story out loud.

ANNA & BLAZER

By _____

One _____ day Anna and her dog, Blazer, went
       1

hiking. They walked to the _____ stream. When they
                   2

became _____, they stopped. Anna sat on a rock.
       3

They listened to the sounds of the _____. Blazer was
                     4

thirsty. Anna _____ him some water from her
       5

canteen. She poured it into a _____ bowl she had

6

carried from home. A fish _____ in the stream. Blazer

7

_____. Soon Anna and Blazer would _____

8   9

home. They wanted to get there before _____.

10

The End

Word Lists

(1) sunny, hot, beautiful, fine, spring, warm, cool, bright, summer, cloudy, clear, pretty

(2) deep, wet, muddy, cool, rippling, shallow, cold, babbling, clear

(3) tired, warm, thirsty, hungry, hot, sleepy

(4) birds, water, frogs, animals, stream, fish, wind, robins

(5) gave, offered, poured, handed

(6) round, plastic, tiny, tin, large, small, dog, water

(7) appeared, jumped, swam, danced, floated, splashed

(8) watched, barked, jumped, swam, ran, sat, drank, slept

(9) walk, hike, run, head, travel, jog, stroll, go, wander, return

(10) night, dark, morning, bedtime, lunch, sundown, six o'clock, dinner, Thursday

Look carefully at the picture below. Then follow the instructions on the next page.

Now answer the following questions. Write your answers on the lines provided.

What animals are in the picture? Where are they?

_____

_____

How are the elephant and the giraffe alike? _____

_____

_____

How are the elephant and the giraffe different? _____

_____

_____

What do giraffes eat? How do you know? _____

_____

_____

If you could have one of these animals as a pet in your home, which one would you have? Where would it sleep?

_____

_____

_____

_____

_____

Use your own words and your imagination to finish the story below. Then read your completed story out loud.

IF I WERE AN ANIMAL

By _____

If I could be an animal, I would be a _____.

I would be covered with _____. My skin would feel

_____. My face would have _____. My

_____ would help me move from place to place.

My _____ would protect me from _____.

As an _____, I would live _____. At
        (animal)

night I would _____. During the day I would

_____. My favorite food would be _____. I

would _____ to get food.

My best friend would be _____. Every day we

would _____ together.

The End

Now draw a picture of yourself as the animal you just described. Be sure to show where you live, as well as some of your friends.

drawn by _____

Fill in the blanks to tell a story. Use a word (or words) from the Word Lists on the next page that matches the number under each blank. Or you might want to write one of your own words! When you are finished, read your whole story again.

A FARM LIFE

By _____

Edward and his _____ live on a farm. Every morning
                        1

before _____, he feeds the _____. Then he
            2   3

collects the _____. The cow is about to have a
                 4

_____. When she is
     5

ready, she will stay in the

_____ until her baby
     6

is born.

The End

Word Lists

(1) brother, goats, pets, sisters, family, aunt and uncle, dogs, horses

(2) school, work, breakfast, showering, brushing his teeth, the sun rises, five o'clock

(3) cows, pigs, goats, animals, chickens, dogs, pets, horses

(4) flowers, trash, oranges, eggs, chickens, berries, mail

(5) meal, carrot, baby, bath, walk, calf, haircut

(6) hospital, field, barn, house, chicken coop, stable

Draw a picture to go with your story.

drawn by

What do you already know about animals? Find out by filling in the blanks. You can use the animals named in the Word Box, or you can pick another animal on your own.

- An animal I could hold on my lap is a _____.
- I could put a saddle on a _____ and ride it.
- A _____ hops across the grass.
- We can find many _____ in the ocean.

- I could walk a _____ on a leash.
- Most of my friends can run faster than a _____.
- My friend Irma keeps a _____ in a cage.
- Sometimes I hear _____ before I see them.
- An animal that moves very slowly is a _____.
- I wouldn't want to make any _____ angry!

Word Box

hamster	cows	frog	crickets	fish
rabbit	turtle	cat	horse	whales
monkey	sharks	birds	bees	snail

Read the instructions on the left side of the page. Then draw pictures in the boxes on the right side of the page to go with each instruction. Be sure to draw a different animal for each instruction.

Draw your favorite animal.

Draw a noisy animal.

Draw the biggest animal you have ever seen.

Draw a funny-looking animal.

Look carefully at the picture below. Then follow the instructions on the next page.

Answer these questions about the picture. Write your answers on the lines.

What kinds of things can you find at the pet store? _____

_____

_____

If you want a new kitten, what should you do to get ready

to take this pet home? _____

_____

_____

What is the man in the picture doing? _____

_____

Would you like to work in a pet store? Why or why not?

_____

_____

Can you think of names for all the animals in the picture?

Write the names here. _____

_____

_____

Write a sentence for each picture to help tell a story. Then read your finished story out loud.

_____

_____

_____

_____

_____

_____

_____

_____

_____

_____

_____

_____

_____

_____

_____

_____

_____

_____

_____

_____

_____

_____

_____

_____

Draw pictures to help tell the story written below.

Some birds built a nest in a tree near Sonya's window.

Sonya watched the mother bird sit on her eggs.

One day a big gust of wind blew the nest to the ground.

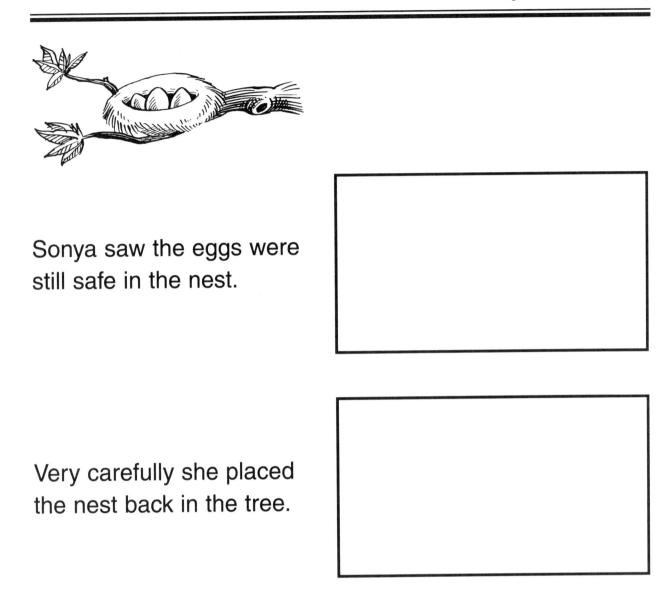

Sonya saw the eggs were still safe in the nest.

Very carefully she placed the nest back in the tree.

Two days later three tiny little birds popped their heads out of the eggshells.

Look at the picture story below. Then draw a picture to tell how the story ends.

Many writers use comparisons to make their writing more interesting. A **comparison** shows how two things are alike or different. Read this example. It compares a koala to a teddy bear. **A koala is as cute as a teddy bear.**

Finish these sentences. Use your imagination to make fun comparisons of your own.

A bunny rabbit is as soft as _____.

A cheetah can run as fast as

_____.

An elephant is bigger than _____.

A snake is as quiet as _____.

A kitten is as gentle as _____.

A flea is as tiny as _____.

Look at the picture below. Then use your own words to finish each sentence.

If I were in this park, I would see _____

_____.

If I were in this park, I would feel _____

_____.

If I were in this park, I would hear _____

_____.

If I were in this park, I would taste _____

_____.

If I were in this park, I would smell _____

_____.

Look at the picture below. Then use your own words to finish each sentence.

If I were under the water, I would see _____

_____.

If I were under the water, I would feel _____

_____.

If I were under the water, I would hear _____

_____.

If I were under the water, I would taste _____

_____.

If I were under the water, I would smell _____

_____.

Look carefully at the picture below. Then follow the instructions on the facing page.

Fill in the blanks to complete the story. Then give your story a title. When you are finished, read your story again.

_____
(title goes here)

By _____

In China this giant panda _____ in the wild. She has been moved to a zoo in the United States.

Giant pandas are very _____ animals. Their fur is black and white. Their black ears and black eye patches make them look _____, no matter how _____ they grow!

Pandas have a favorite food. They _____ to eat bamboo. At the zoo the panda's _____ is filled with bamboo. She can _____ the rocks and _____ in the pond.

I want to give the giant panda a name. Since she is so _____, I will name her _____.

The End

Look carefully at the picture below. Then follow the instructions on the next page.

Fill in the blanks to complete the story. Then give your story a title. When you are finished, read your story again.

_____
(title goes here)

By _____

The captain stopped the boat. He turned off the motor.

"Good morning," he said in a loud voice. "Welcome. My name is Captain _____. This is my boat. I named my boat _____.

"I have a feeling we will see some _____ today. Keep your _____ open. This time of year, they _____ in these waters looking for _____. Last week we saw _____."

Maria asked a question. "Do they ever come too close to _____?" She was a little _____.

"Only when we are _____," said the captain.

"Look over there!" shouted William. "I see a _____!"

The End

The next few stories have a beginning and a middle. Use what you read in the story and your imagination to write an ending to each story.

A PET FOR AMELIA

By _____

"Dad, please may I have a pet?"

It was Saturday morning. Amelia and her dad sat at the breakfast table. Amelia poured milk on her cereal. Her father bit into a peach. He had heard this question 20 times before. The answer was always the same.

"Amelia, you know our apartment building doesn't allow dogs. And cats make me sick. My eyes itch and I sneeze. Besides, you are too young to take care of a pet by yourself."

Amelia scraped the cereal from the side of her bowl. Yes, it was the same answer. She kept hoping that one day his answer would be different.

"I'm seven now," she said. "I take care of what I am supposed to. I do the dinner dishes. I sort all of the laundry. I know I could take care of a pet."

Her dad was silent for a long time. Suddenly,

he smiled. "I have an idea," he said. "After breakfast,
let's _____

_____

_____

_____

_____

_____

_____

_____

_____

_____

The End

Draw a picture to show the ending of your story.

drawn by _____

GUIDE DOGS

By _____

Have you ever entered a store with this sign?

> **No Animals**
> **Except**
> **Guide Dogs**

Do you know what guide dogs are? Guide dogs are dogs that help people who cannot see at all or who cannot see well. These dogs live with their owners and "guide" them to the places they need to go.

Guide dogs are very special. They must be kind, gentle, and well-behaved dogs. After they are chosen to be guide dogs, they begin "school." They learn to obey special orders, like "left," "right," and "forward." They also learn not to jump at loud noises. Guide dogs must always remain calm. After all, a guide dog's job is to lead its owner.

One of the most important things they learn is to STOP. A guide dog must stop any time the path changes. A curb, a step, a rock, or even a puddle can cause the owner to stumble. When the guide

dog stops, it will either go a different way, or wait for its owner to discover the change and give the order to go.

After school, the guide dog and its new owner train together. With the help of a special trainer, the guide dog and new owner practice in the real world. They might practice going to the owner's job. They might practice getting on and off a bus. They might practice going to the store or other places the owner needs to go each day.

They get to know each other. After about one month, the guide dog and its new owner are ready to live on their own.

Guide dogs can be very important to their owners. Some things that a blind person can do with the help of a guide dog are _____

_____

_____

_____

_____

_____

_____

_____

_____

_____

_____

The End

DIARY OF A YOUNG BEAGLE

By _____

November 1995

Dear Diary,

My name is Daisy and I am a beagle. I live with my human family in a house in the country. There are two children in my family. Their names are Jenna and Matt. They go to school almost every day, so I sleep a lot. My favorite place to sleep is a big old chair. None of the people in my family sit in that chair. Only me. If I sit on another chair, my family says, "Go to your own chair, Daisy!"

February 1996

Dear Diary,

We're moving to the city! Jenna and Matt's mother told them that we are all going to move when school is over in June. I wonder what the city will be like. I wonder if there are other dogs in the city. I wonder _____

_____

_____

_____

_____

Write Daisy's next journal entry. It can be before or after she and her family move to the city. It's up to you!

_____
(date)

Dear Diary,

_____

_____

_____

_____

_____

_____

_____

_____

Now draw a picture of Daisy in her new home.

drawn by _____

BEWARE OF THE HANDSTAND

By _____

What animal strikes fear in brave mountain lions and ferocious bears, even though it is the size of a puppy? Do you give up? The answer is a skunk.

The skunk doesn't run very fast. It doesn't have very sharp claws, a strong grasp, or a painful bite. Instead, the skunk has a very unusual, powerful weapon—the horrible smell of its spray!

The disgusting odor of its spray is the skunk's protection from danger. It sprays at its enemies or when it feels frightened.

Have you ever seen a skunk do a handstand? If you do, RUN! This means the skunk is getting ready to spray. The spray comes from two pouches under the skunk's tail. When it stands on its hands, the skunk is taking aim!

Imagine you are in a park with your friends. You smell the odor of a skunk's spray. What might have happened?

_____

_____

_____

_____

_____

_____

The End

Use the lines below to tell a story about this skunk.

_____

(title goes here)

By _____

_____
_____
_____
_____
_____
_____
_____
_____

_____
_____
_____
_____
_____
_____
_____
_____

The End

A LETTER FROM AUSTRALIA

Robert Juarez
123 Flower Street, Apt. 106
Teaneck, New Jersey

July 1, 1996

Dear Robert,

I am having a great vacation in Australia. The people are really nice. The cities are beautiful. We even got to see real koalas!

We had to drive to a preserve to see the koalas. Preserves are special areas where the koalas are protected. I knew we were almost there when I saw a sign that said:

Finally I got my first good look at a real koala. It was the cutest animal I've ever seen. It looked like a teddy bear, but even cuter. No wonder people think koalas are bears, but they are not. They are marsupials. Marsupials are animals that carry their newborn babies in a pouch. Kangaroos are also marsupials.

We saw a mother koala, but we couldn't see her baby. When they are first born, the babies stay inside the pouch. They grow there until they are big enough to come out into the world.

I can't wait to see you! Please write me at the address on the envelope.

Your friend,
Brooke

Now pretend you are Brooke's friend Robert. Write a letter to Brooke telling her how you spent your vacation. Did you see any adorable or amazing animals?

_____

_____

_____

_____

_____

_____

_____

_____

_____

_____

_____

_____

_____

The stories that follow have a beginning and an ending. But they are missing their middle parts! Use what you read and your imagination to write the middle parts for each story.

DANNY THE DORMOUSE

By _____

In autumn the forest animals are busy. Danny the Dormouse and his friends scurry from tree to tree looking for nuts and seeds to eat.

Danny has to eat a lot and makes himself really fat. He is getting ready for a **long** nap. You see, dormice like Danny sleep all the way from the fall until the spring!

Danny likes to sleep. But lately he's been wondering what he misses during his long winter nap. Other animals talk about winter and snow. Danny has never seen snow, and he is very curious about winter.

This fall Danny the Dormouse has made a new plan. He is going to _____

_____

_____

_____

_____

_____

Three Months Later . . .

Danny has never been so tired in his whole life! But he doesn't mind. He just can't wait for his friends to wake up so he can tell them all about his adventures. And he can't wait to find more food. But most of all, he can't wait to take a long nap!

The End

Draw a picture of Danny the Dormouse in the forest, getting ready for the winter.

drawn by _____

OLIVER

By _____

There once was an otter named Oliver. He lived with his family on the river. Every day Oliver paddled his strong, heavy tail through the water. He loved to swim. He loved to find fish to eat. But most of all, Oliver loved to play.

One day Oliver suddenly spotted a great new place to play. It was a mud slide at the edge of the water! Oliver quickly gathered his brothers, sisters, and friends and led them to the mud slide.

Slip! Swish! Splash! _____

_____

_____

_____

_____

_____

_____

_____

_____

Oliver started to feel tired and hungry. It was beginning to get dark. He knew it was time to stop playing. So Oliver and his brothers, sisters, and friends all swam home.

The End

Draw Oliver in the picture of the river. Then draw any other otters that you wrote about in the story.

MY JOB

By _____

My name is Rebecca Johnson. I have the best job in the world. I take care of the chimpanzees at the zoo. I feed them and play with them. I make sure their homes, called **habitats,** are clean and safe. Sometimes I just watch them.

Since I was a child, I knew I wanted to work with animals. I always _____

_____

_____

_____

_____

_____

_____

_____

_____

My hero is Jane Goodall. She spent over 30 years studying chimpanzees in Africa. She learned to know when chimps are sick or sad. She convinced zoos to make life safe and healthy for chimps. Because of her work, chimpanzees have better and happier lives in zoos.

The End

Draw a picture to go with the story.

drawn by ✏ _____

ASK THE ZOOKEEPER

By _____

Dear Zookeeper at Bailey's Zoo,

My friends and I can't agree. What is the fastest running animal in the world? I think it is a big cat, like a leopard, but they think a giraffe can cover ground faster because of its long legs. Can you help us?

Yours truly,
George Johnson

Dear George,

You made the closest guess. The fastest animal on land is the cheetah. The cheetah is one of the big cats. Cheetahs can run faster than racehorses. Some cheetahs run faster than 70 miles an hour. That's faster than the speed limit for cars on our highways!

Sincerely,
The Zookeeper at Bailey's Zoo

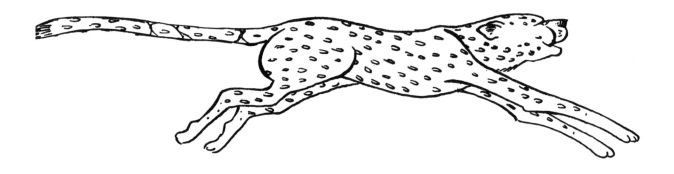

Dear Zookeeper at Bailey's Zoo,

_____

_____

_____

_____

_____

_____

_____

_____

Dear _____,

You will be surprised to learn that, yes, the electric eel really does have electrical energy. The electrical power we use in our homes is 120 volts. An electric eel can make 650 volts of electrical power! That's enough to kill small fish and stun larger animals so they cannot move. But there's no need for you to worry at your local beach. This kind of eel lives only in South American rivers.

Sincerely,
The Zookeeper at Bailey's Zoo

Do you have a question about an animal? Use the lines below to write your question in a letter.

_____

_____

_____

_____

_____

_____

_____

_____

_____

Draw a picture to go with your letter.

drawn by _____

FINDING FIFI

By _____

David's telephone rang.

"Quick," his friend Ronald said. "Come to my house. Mrs. Chen's dog, Fifi, is missing. We have got to help find her."

"I'll be over in ten minutes," said David. "I'll stop and get Marina. She will want to help Mrs. Chen, too."

David was right about his friend Marina. "Of course I'll help," she said. "Let me get my sweater. Oh, and I'll bring my markers and some pieces of cardboard."

_____

_____

_____

_____

_____

_____

_____

_____

_____

_____

_____

_____

_____
_____
_____
_____
_____
_____
_____
_____
_____
_____
_____
_____
_____
_____
_____
_____

Mrs. Chen cuddled Fifi on her lap. Fifi was muddy, but Mrs. Chen didn't mind.

"I am really lucky," Mrs. Chen said to David, Ronald, and Marina, "to have such caring friends like you."

The End

Draw three pictures to illustrate the story "Finding Fifi." Show what happened at the beginning of the story, what happened in the middle, and what happened at the end.

Read this story. Then complete the sentences on the facing page.

PENGUINS

By _____

People think penguins are very cute. Their colors make them look like they are dressed up in fancy suits called tuxedos. But don't be fooled by their cute looks. Penguins are strong and sturdy! They have to be strong. They live in the coldest places in the world.

The biggest kinds of penguins are called emperor penguins. Emperor penguins usually have one baby at a time. The job of taking care of the baby is shared by the mother and the father.

First the mother lays the egg. Then she passes the egg—as fast as she can—to the father. They have to do this very fast so the egg won't freeze in the cold air. The father puts the egg in a special place called a brood pouch between his tummy and his foot. There, the egg stays warm and safe until it is ready to hatch.

The End

Many writers use comparisons to make their writing more fun. A **comparison** shows how two things are alike or different. Finish each sentence below by making a comparison.

Penguins are so cute. They look like _____.

A penguin's feathers grow close together to make a thick coat. The feathers keep them warm just like _____.

Penguins must be as strong as _____ to live where it is very cold.

Instead of wings, penguins have fins for swimming. Penguins swim in the water just like _____.

In the father's brood pouch, the egg is as warm as _____.

Write your own comparison here:

_____

_____

_____

Use the words in the Word Box below to write your own story. Be sure to give your story a beginning, a middle, and an ending. Remember that the beginning tells what the story is about. The middle tells a problem. The ending tells how the problem is solved. Then give your story a title.

After you write your own story, read it again. Make any changes or corrections you want.

Word Box

squirrel   silly   lazy   nuts

monkey   bright   forgot   tree

_____

(title goes here)

By _____

_____

_____

_____

_____

_____

_____

_____

_____

_____

_____

_____

_____

_____

_____

_____

_____

_____

_____

_____

_____

_____

_____

_____

_____

_____

_____

_____

_____ .

The End

Now draw pictures to go with your story. Show what happened in the beginning, what happened in the middle, and what happened at the end of your story.

What do you know about dinosaurs? Write a story of your own about something that happened when dinosaurs lived. You can make yourself a dinosaur, or you can pretend you are the only person living with dinosaurs. Use your imagination. Give your story a beginning, a middle, and an ending. Then give your story a title.

    After you write your story, read it again. Make any changes or corrections you want.

_____

(title goes here)

By _____

_____

_____

_____

_____

_____

_____

_____

_____

_____

_____

_____

_____

The End

Draw pictures to go with your dinosaur story. Show what happened in the beginning, what happened in the middle, and what happened at the end of your story.

Scientists study animals carefully. They want to learn how animals move. Many scientists work together to make machines, such as robots, to imitate animals.

Look at the diagram of an airplane. In what ways is an airplane like a bird? _____

_____

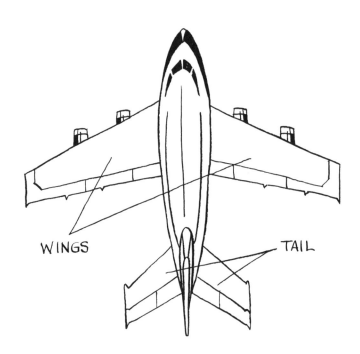

WINGS   TAIL

Now imagine you are a scientist. Your job is to make an animal robot. What would it be like if a robot could run as fast as a cheetah? Or jump as far as a frog jumps?

Choose something an animal does that is very special. How could you make a robot that imitates that animal? Tell what you want your robot to do and how you might make the robot. What would you name your robot?

Write a story about your own animal robot. Give your story a beginning, a middle, and an ending. Then give your story a title.

   After you write your story, read it again to make any changes or corrections you want.

_____

(title goes here)

By _____

_____

_____

_____

_____

_____

_____

_____

_____

_____

_____

_____

_____

_____

_____

The End

A **diagram** like the one on page 60 is a drawing that shows how something is made or how it works. Draw a diagram of your animal robot. Write labels where they are needed.

drawn by _____